BRAIN

FIND THE KITTEN

Publications International, Ltd.

Images from Shutterstock.com

Brain Games is a registered trademark of Publications International, Ltd.

Copyright © 2023 Publications International, Ltd. All rights reserved. This book may not be reproduced or quoted in whole or in part by any means whatsoever without written permission from:

Louis Weber, CEO
Publications International, Ltd.
8140 Lehigh Avenue
Morton Grove, IL 60053

Permission is never granted for commercial purposes.

ISBN: 978-1-63938-214-9

Manufactured in China.

8 7 6 5 4 3 2 1

Here, Kitty Kitty!

Ready for a unique, picture-based puzzle book filled with furtive felines? This book contains adorable kittens that have snuck onto the pages of every scene—and your job is to find them. Each picture holds a single kitty. Carefully scan each photo—remember, mischievous kittens can get just about everywhere. While it's fun to search for these furry friends, it can still be difficult. If you get stumped, you can always peek at the answers at the back of the book.

Answer on page 130.

Answer on page 130.

Answer on page 130.

Answer on page 130.

Answer on page 130.

Answer on page 131.

Answer on page 131.

Answer on page 131.

Answer on page 131.

Answer on page 132.

Answer on page 132.

Answer on page 132.

Answer on page 133.

Answer on page 133.

Answer on page 133.

Answer on page 133.

Answer on page 134.

Answer on page 134.

Answer on page 134.

Answer on page 135.

Answer on page 135.

Answer on page 135.

Answer on page 135.

Answer on page 136.

Answer on page 136.

Answer on page 136.

Answer on page 136.

Answer on page 137.

Answer on page 137.

Answer on page 137.

Answer on page 137.

38

Answer on page 138.

Answer on page 138.

Answer on page 138.

Answer on page 139.

Answer on page 139.

Answer on page 139.

Answer on page 139.

Answer on page 140.

Answer on page 140.

Answer on page 140.

Answer on page 141.

Answer on page 141.

Answer on page 141.

Answer on page 142.

Answer on page 142.

Answer on page 142.

Answer on page 142.

Answer on page 143.

59

Answer on page 143.

Answer on page 143.

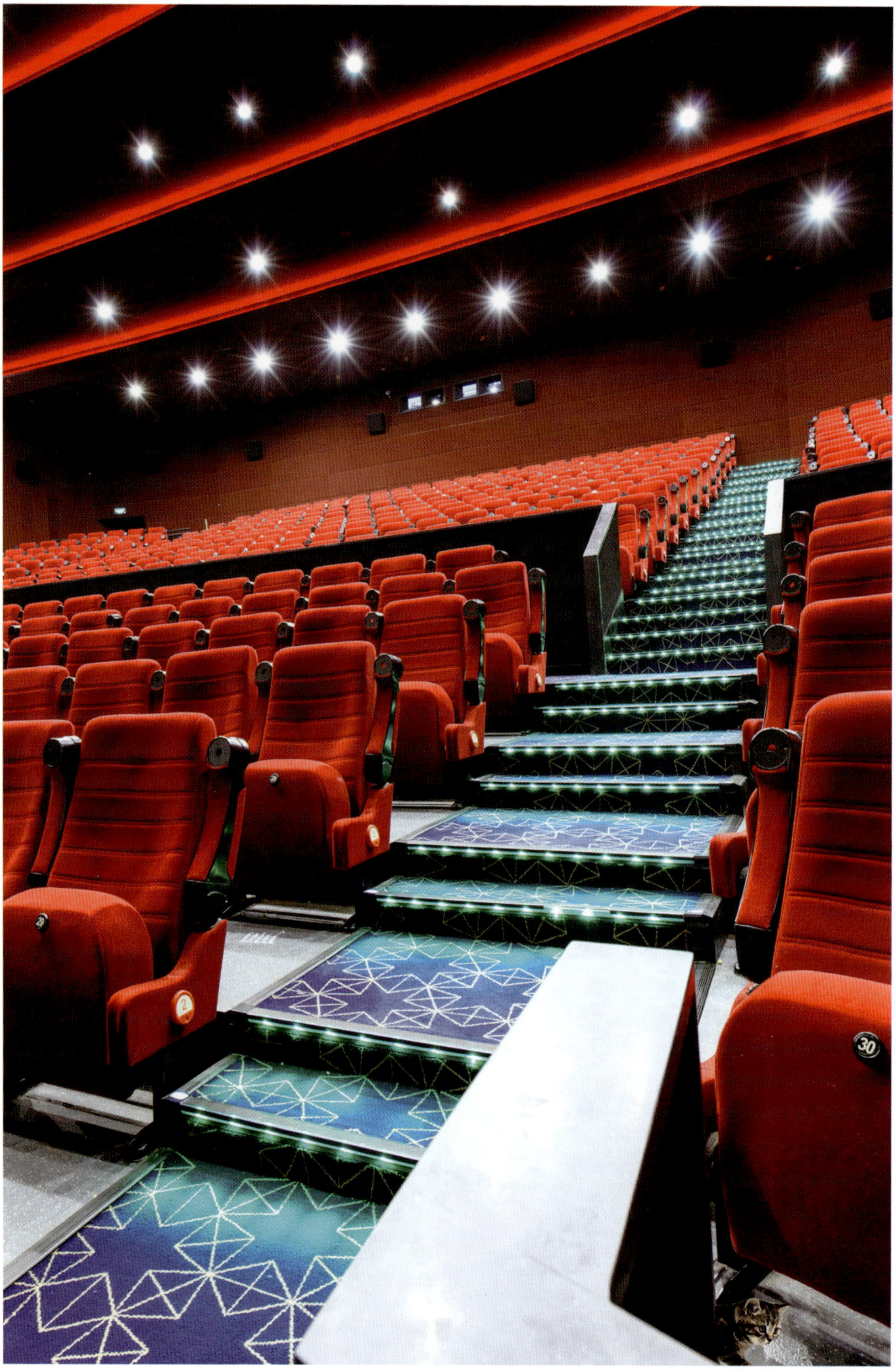

Answer on page 144.

Answer on page 144.

Answer on page 144.

Answer on page 144.

Answer on page 145.

Answer on page 145.

Answer on page 145.

Answer on page 145.

Answer on page 146.

Answer on page 146.

Answer on page 146.

Answer on page 146.

Answer on page 147.

Answer on page 147.

Answer on page 147.

Answer on page 147.

78

Answer on page 148.

Answer on page 148.

Answer on page 148.

Answer on page 149.

Answer on page 149.

Answer on page 149.

Answer on page 150.

Answer on page 150.

Answer on page 150.

Answer on page 151.

Answer on page 151.

Answer on page 151.

Answer on page 151.

Answer on page 152.

Answer on page 152.

96

Answer on page 152.

Answer on page 152.

Answer on page 153.

Answer on page 153.

100

Answer on page 153.

Answer on page 153.

Answer on page 154.

Answer on page 154.

Answer on page 154.

Answer on page 154.

Answer on page 155.

108

Answer on page 155.

Answer on page 155.

Answer on page 156.

Answer on page 156.

Answer on page 156.

Answer on page 157.

Answer on page 157.

Answer on page 157.

Answer on page 157.

Answer on page 158.

Answer on page 158.

Answer on page 158.

Answer on page 159.

Answer on page 159.

Answer on page 159.

Answer on page 160.

Answer on page 160.

128

Answer on page 160.

ANSWERS

Page 4

Page 6

Page 8

Page 5

Page 7

Page 9

Page 10

Page 11

Page 12

Page 13

Page 14

Page 16

Page 15

Page 17

Page 18

Page 19

Page 20

Page 21

Page 22

Page 23

Page 24

Page 25

ANSWERS

Page 26

Page 27

Page 28

Page 29

ANSWERS

Page 30

Page 31

Page 32

Page 33

ANSWERS

Page 34

Page 35

Page 36

Page 37

Page 38

Page 39

Page 40

Page 41

ANSWERS

Page 42

Page 44

Page 43

Page 45

Page 46

Page 47

Page 48

Page 49

ANSWERS

Page 50

Page 51

Page 52

Page 53

ANSWERS

Page 54

Page 55

Page 56

Page 57

Page 58

Page 59

Page 60

Page 61

Page 62

Page 63

Page 64

Page 65

Page 66

Page 67

Page 68

Page 69

ANSWERS

Page 70

Page 71

Page 72

Page 73

ANSWERS

Page 74

Page 75

Page 76

Page 77

ANSWERS

Page 78

Page 79

Page 80

Page 81

ANSWERS

Page 82

Page 83

Page 84

Page 85

Page 86

Page 88

Page 87

Page 89

ANSWERS

Page 90

Page 91

Page 92

Page 93

151

ANSWERS

Page 94

Page 95

Page 96

Page 97

Page 98

Page 99

Page 100

Page 101

ANSWERS

Page 102

Page 103

Page 104

Page 105

ANSWERS

Page 106

Page 107

Page 108

Page 109

ANSWERS

Page 110

Page 111

Page 112

Page 113

Page 114

Page 115

Page 116

Page 117

Page 118

Page 119

Page 120

Page 121

Page 122

Page 123

Page 124

Page 125

ANSWERS

Page 126

Page 127

Page 128

Page 129